DEPARTMENT STORES

Claire

SHIRE PUBLICATIONS

Published in Great Britain in 2013 by Shire Publications Ltd,
Midland House, West Way, Botley, Oxford OX2 0PH,
United Kingdom.
4301 21st St, Suite 220B, Long Island City, NY 11101,
USA.

E-mail: shire@shirebooks.co.uk   www.shirebooks.co.uk

Every attempt has been made by the Publishers to secure
the appropriate permissions for materials reproduced in
this book. If there has been any oversight we will be happy
to rectify the situation and a written submission should be
made to the Publishers.

A CIP catalogue record for this book is available from the
British Library.

Shire Library no. 588   •   ISBN-13: 978 0 74780 772 8

Claire Masset has asserted her right under the Copyright,
Designs and Patents Act, 1988, to be identified as the
author of this book.

Designed by Tony Truscott Designs, Sussex, UK
and typeset in Perpetua and Gill Sans.
Printed in China through World Print Ltd.

13 14 15 16 17   12 11 10 9 8 7 6 5 4 3

COVER IMAGE
The Department Store, illustration from 'Cours
Schweiter', c. 1900

TITLE PAGE IMAGE
The full-colour cover of the Jones Bros 1912 Summer Sale
catalogue.

CONTENTS PAGE IMAGE
A print showing Bainbridge & Co. in the 1890s. By this
time, the store stretched over two streets and 'across the
rear of sixteen other business establishments'. Note the
Bainbridge signs on the roofs in the background and the
Bainbridge delivery carts in the foreground.

ACKNOWLEDGEMENTS
With thanks to Lesley and David Beange, Frank Boyle,
Maggie Cammiss, Brian Carter, Judy Faraday, Judi James,
Thomas Macey, Linda Moroney, Susan Payne, Sarah
Pearson, Ingrid Ramm-Bonwitt, Kevin Sinclair and Nick
Wright. Special thanks to Alex and Gavin Toone, Betty
Gash and Sarah Masset for their help and patience.

Illustrations are acknowledged as follows:

Archives Charmet/Bridgeman Art Library, cover; David
Beange, page 57; Frank Boyle, page 51 (bottom);
Bridgeman Art Library, page 19 (top); Debenhams Plc,
pages 54 and 60; Fenwick's, pages 18 (top), 24 (bottom),
and 42; Getty Images, pages 4 and 40; Harvey Nichols,
pages 61 (bottom) and 62 (top); Jacksons of Reading,
page 16; John Lewis Partnership, pages 1, 3, 9, 19
(bottom), 30, 32, 34 (top), 35 (bottom), 38 (bottom),
43 (bottom), 44 (both), 45, 48 (both), 49 (both), 50
(both), 53, and 56 (bottom); Mary Evans, pages 6, 22, 39
(top); McEwens of Perth, page 10; Perth Museum & Art
Gallery, page 38 (top); Selfridges, pages 24 (top), 56 (top),
and 59; Kevin Sinclair, page 62 (bottom); The Stapleton
Collection/Bridgeman Art Library, page 11. All other
pictures are taken from Claire Masset's personal
collection.

Shire Publications is supporting the Woodland Trust, the UK's leading woodland conservation charity, by funding the dedication of trees.

BAINBRIDGE & CO., Drapery and House Furnishing Warehousemen,

29, 31, 33, 35, & 37, Market Street, and 26 & 28, Bigg Market, Newcastle.

CONTENTS

INTRODUCTION   5

ORIGINS AND BEGINNINGS   7

LIFE AND SPECTACLE IN STORE   23

THE POST-WAR ERA   41

TODAY'S STORE   55

FURTHER READING   63

INDEX   64

INTRODUCTION

Enticing windows, dazzling Christmas displays and queues of avid shoppers during the sales – these are just some of the images conjured up by the term 'department store'. Some of us remember the thrill of visiting a luxury London store, such as Harrods, Selfridges or Liberty. Others have fond memories of much-anticipated trips to a local store, with its helpful sales assistants and warren of inviting departments. Whatever your recollection, department stores carry a sense of history tinged with nostalgia.

From its beginnings in the 1850s through its golden age in the early twentieth century to its more recent and chequered past, the history of the department store is as wonderful as it is revealing. For a place that trades on offering an escape from the rigours of daily life, it is, surprisingly, a fascinating barometer for social change. The story of the department store reflects many of the major developments that we have witnessed in our lifetime, from innovations in fashion, technology and design to the increasing importance of retailing, marketing and the changing world of work. Harrods was one of the very first retailers to introduce 24-hour telephone shopping. Selfridges, always at the cutting-edge of retail, was the first store to sell telephones and television sets. Lewis's of Liverpool was one of the first businesses to understand the advantages of central buying. And, in 1924, way ahead of its time, Howells of Cardiff started selling cars in a specially designed showroom.

As well as reflecting contemporary developments, department stores have, at times, helped shape the course of history. It has been argued that the department store played a key role in the emancipation of women, acting as a safe place in which to meet friends outside the home, but also offering many work opportunities, at a time when there were few attractive openings for women.

Beyond what they tell us about our social history, department stores were, and indeed still are, amazing places, acting not just as shops, but as meeting places, restaurants and sometimes museums. Today, there is at least one department store in every British city. But imagine a world without them. This was the case just 200 years ago.

Opposite:
This evocative 1916 photograph shows two uniformed lift operators at Swan & Edgar's department store in London. Note the S&E monogram on the carpet.

ORIGINS AND BEGINNINGS

SHOPPING is so much part of our lives that we almost take it for granted. For centuries, however, shopping simply meant buying from local markets and small shops, or directly from craftsmen and street traders. Until the Elizabethan age, most towns relied on a weekly market and on larger but less frequent fairs. For the majority of people, shopping was about self-sufficiency not self-indulgence. Shops, if there were any, were simply open windows with a drop-down counter on which wares were shown to customers. From the sixteenth century, shopkeeping slowly developed as a trade in itself, with shopkeepers shouting their wares beside the board or in the street. It was only in the eighteenth century that shops became grander and more elaborate. Some of them then started offering elegant showrooms (sometimes called 'ware rooms') where customers could browse at leisure and items were artistically displayed. At the same time, enticing new glazed shop fronts, some of which projected out into the street, also appeared. The terms 'shopping for pleasure' and 'window-shopping' were just around the corner.

But what led to these changes in shops and shopping habits? And how did some of these new shops develop into fully-fledged department stores? The first reason is economic. Thanks mainly to the Industrial Revolution, over the course of the eighteenth and nineteenth centuries people were better fed and housed, and, significantly, had more money to spend. A new middle class was emerging, keen to indulge in 'conspicuous consumption'. Alongside this rise in spending power came phenomenal urban growth throughout Britain. In just fifty years, London's population almost quadrupled from about 1 million in 1809 to 3.8 million in 1861. While Manchester's inhabitants numbered 17,000 in 1758, by 1851 the total had reached 300,000. Between 1801 and 1891, urban dwellers in England and Wales had increased from 2.3 million to a staggering 19.8 million.

The department store, a city-centre phenomenon, appeared in the context of this rapidly growing – and more accessible – urban world. The rail and road networks were developing fast. By 1870, 13,000 miles of railway

Opposite:
This Harrods advert from 1897 lists a total of eighty different departments.

track had been laid, thereby revolutionising the distribution of consumer goods and enabling more people to travel longer distances. The first section of the London Underground opened in 1863; within a few months it was carrying over 25,000 passengers a day.

As historian Sir Roy Strong puts it: 'More people, more money, more means whereby to transport them, and everywhere as a consequence shops and stores multiplied.' Up until the 1830s, shops tended to be specialised. There were bookshops, china shops, chemists, confectioners, cabinetmakers, boot and shoe dealers, jewellers, silk mercers, drapers, grocers, ironmongers, bakers, butchers and so on. But in the mid-nineteenth century, one particular class of retailer – the draper – outgrew all others, gradually expanding his premises and range of products. An exciting new breed of shop, today described as the 'proto-department store', had appeared.

Drapers had a lot going for them, not least the requirements of fashion. The new crinoline craze, endorsed by the young Queen Victoria and the

An 1860s print displaying the contemporary fashion for wide skirts. Requiring excessive amounts of fabric, the crinoline made many a draper's fortune and was a key factor in the rise of the department store.

Empress Eugénie of France, required unprecedented amounts of fabric to create the 'billowing' and cumbersome skirt. Although criticised by social reformers and ridiculed by the satirical press, this type of dress was a goldmine for the draper. Each outfit required yards of fabric for the outer skirt, as well as material for three, sometimes even four, petticoats and for the accompanying paraphernalia, including cotton or silk underwear and muslin shifts.

GENTLEMEN'S TAILORING DEPARTMENT.

Fashion wasn't the only reason for the success of the drapery trade. While shopkeepers relied on a risky but time-honoured credit system, new retailers started demanding payment upfront, or 'ready money'. Hand in hand with this ready-money policy went clearly marked prices, another novelty in those days. In 1831 Jolly & Son of Bath was one of the very first stores to introduce fixed prices, announcing: 'There will be no abatement made from the price asked, the profit on each article being too small to admit any reduction.'

By 1893, Bainbridge's had branched out into clothing and boasted a 'Gentlemen's Tailoring Department', as this print illustrates.

The ready-money system enabled retailers to pay their suppliers in cash and get better and bigger deals. This, together with a high demand for cloth and a greatly improved distribution network, helped drapers to increase their turnover, which in turn meant that they could invest in new and more varied stock and also offer lower prices, usually 15 to 20 per cent cheaper than those found in other retailers.

Perhaps the most successful proto-department store was Bainbridge's, a drapery founded in Newcastle in 1838. Emerson Muschamp Bainbridge sold good-quality products much more cheaply than his rivals and insisted on cash payment. By 1849, his weekly takings were recorded by department, of which there were already twenty-three. The shop started selling gloves, stockings, bags and other clothing-related items. A similar story can be seen at Kendal, Milne & Faulkner, a drapery partnership established in Manchester in 1836. By 1847, the store had expanded its range of products and services to include furniture, upholstery and even funeral undertaking.

Across the country, enterprising drapery retailers were quickly expanding their range of products. Arnott & Co. in Glasgow, which opened as a drapery shop in about 1850, soon started offering ready-made coats, trousers and other clothing, as well as carpets, haberdashery and all sorts of accessories, such as shawls and parasols. By 1864, it described itself as 'the

A photograph of McEwens in Perth dating from the early twentieth century. From selling small items of clothing and accessories, the store expanded to supply tailor-made outfits for men and women. In those days, all counter assistants were men, while women worked as seamstresses.

largest retail drapery in the city'. Cavendish House in Cheltenham opened as a drapery business in 1823; by 1872 it boasted over twenty departments. By 1894 Barkers in Kensington comprised sixty-four departments and employed 1,500 staff. Howells of Cardiff, Jenners and Maule's of Edinburgh, John Lewis and D. H. Evans of Oxford Street, Binns of Sunderland, Brown Muff & Co. of Bradford, McEwens of Perth, Chiesman's of Lewisham, Debenham & Freebody of Wigmore Street and countless other department stores all started life as drapers.

The insistence on cash payments coupled with fixed prices helped make shopping more accessible to the newly wealthy middle classes. With no more haggling and clear price tags, shopping was now more straightforward.

The Victorian age is often regarded as the dawn of consumerism. The middle classes were keen to show off their new wealth through possessions and, thanks to advances in technology and manufacturing, there was a greater variety of products from which to choose. With its stunning displays, the Great Exhibition of 1851 was a vast showroom of worldwide – but particularly British – products. It undoubtedly helped fuel the desire for material goods. Over six million visitors came to see about 100,000 items, including furniture, tapestries, clocks, furs, fabrics, tools, porcelain and glass, displayed in the stunning Crystal Palace building. The Great Exhibition set new standards in the display of manufactured goods. Visitors could explore the different departments enjoying not just the astonishing range of items, but also music and refreshments. It is hardly surprising that the exhibition was described at the time as a 'bazaar' – like a huge shop, except that you couldn't actually buy any of the items.

Retail historians have noted the fact that William Whiteley visited the Great Exhibition as a young man. This event may well have influenced his decision to move from Yorkshire to London to seek his fortune as a retailer. His store, which opened in 1863 in Bayswater's Westbourne Grove, was by the end of the century 'an immense symposium of the arts and industries of the nation and of the world' – much like the Crystal Palace had been during the Great Exhibition.

Concentrating first on drapery stock, by the late 1860s the store featured ladies' clothes, gloves and hosiery, jewellery, furs, umbrellas and artificial flowers. By the mid-1870s, new products and services were added, including dressmaking, tailoring, boots and hats, an estate agency, hairdressing, cleaning and dyeing services, tea rooms and a furniture shop. A canny self-publicist, Whiteley was now dubbing himself 'the Universal Provider' and enjoying much attention in the newspapers. In 1875 he started selling food; in 1876

The Hardware and Woodcarving Machinery section at London's Great Exhibition of 1851. With its extensive range of items displayed artistically in different sections, the Great Exhibition resembled a vast department store.

VUE du HALL CENTRAL des NOUVEAUX MAGASINS DU PRINTEMPS
Ce Hall octogonal, large d'e 25 mètres, est couronné à 50 mètres de hauteur, par
un dôme d'une prodigieuse hardiesse, support d'une éblouissante verrière.

he was offering building and decorating services. By 1881, Whiteley's also sold pictures, pianos, flowers and railway tickets, and boasted an interesting new 'hire' service which offered to source any items required. Some of the particularly unusual requests he received included an elephant, a second-hand coffin and a best man for a wedding!

Opposite: A view of the dazzling central hall of Printemps, as illustrated in a 1910 promotional booklet. Sadly, the cupola is no longer visible from the lower floors.

A 1910 postcard showing customers enjoying the palatial surroundings of the Printemps store. Note the stunning central display of plants on the staircase.

William Whiteley was one of the first retailers to realise the importance of the 'shopping experience', where sumptuous displays and customer service were as important as the goods on offer. This concept actually originated in Paris whose *grands magasins* – including Le Bon Marché, Printemps and Galeries Lafayette – were attracting so much attention that French author Émile Zola wrote a book about the life and spectacle of the department store. In *Au Bonheur des Dames* (*The Ladies' Paradise*), Zola compares the department store to a vast cathedral of commerce and depicts in detail the lavish displays, the lives of the employees and the phenomenal marketing skills of the store's owner. An insightful social commentator, Zola describes department stores as contributing to the 'democratisation of luxury', and he based his book on Le Bon Marché, now considered the world's first department store. Founded in 1852 by Aristide Boucicaut, Le Bon Marché operated according to the then novel practices of fixed and marked prices, small mark-ups, free entrance with no obligation to buy, and an appealing returns policy – principles that were taken up by other department stores, including in Britain, in the second half of the nineteenth century.

The Parisian shops were, and indeed still are, stunning buildings. Partly designed by Gustave Eiffel, Le Bon Marché, with its elegant gold and cream interior, is a joy to visit. Its sweeping staircase (now replaced with a stylish escalator) encouraged the flow of customers and enabled goods to be artistically draped across gallery rails. Galeries Lafayette is famous for its shimmering stained-glass cupola. Here too, as in many other French stores, the galleried storeys create a theatrical effect and offer enticing glimpses of the items for sale on all floors. Many British stores followed this

The Galeries Lafayette store in Paris, photographed in the early twentieth century. Note the headless mannequins and the named departments on the building itself. *Peignoirs* are bathrobes and *layettes* linens.

galleried model, including Jenners of Edinburgh, Fraser's of Glasgow and Liberty of London.

By the 1870s, Paris had become the capital of international shopping and the emerging British department stores were starting to cash in on French style and fashion. Cavendish House of Cheltenham employed agents in Paris to buy all the latest French fashion items. Bon Marché in Liverpool, founded in 1878, was modelled on its Parisian namesake. So too was Brixton's Bon Marché, which opened in 1877. Brown's of Chester went as far as recruiting French sales assistants.

While emerging department stores increased their range of goods, they also considerably expanded their premises. Many of the British stores developed in a piecemeal manner, with showrooms and departments added as adjoining or nearby premises became available. Buildings rose in height as floors were added when necessary. Lewis's of Liverpool, which was founded in 1856, grew so quickly that by 1886 it formed a nine-storey building with frontages on three streets. The same can be said for Barkers, Derry & Toms, and Pontings of Kensington, all of which expanded by acquiring or taking over leases of premises on Kensington High Street. In Central London, Gamages gradually took over numbers 116 to 128 Holborn. The store became a warren

An 1874 print showing the French department store Les Grands Magasins du Pauvre Diable. Featuring a central staircase and galleried storeys, the layout is typical of early department stores and enabled customers to see – and be tempted by – as many goods as possible.

E. JACKSON, King's Road Corners, Reading.

Special attention is called to this rapidly growing Department.

WE ARE REPLETE WITH ALL THE Newest and most Charming Styles for Ladies' Wear.

Tailor-made COATS & SKIRTS
A SPECIALITY.
(Cut and Made on the Premises).

Ladies' Coats and Skirts,
Latest Fashionable Styles,
READY TO WEAR.
21/- 26/- 31/6 42/- 63/-

Ladies' Mantles and Capes,
12/6 to 45/-
Ladies' Raincoats, 10/6 to 35/-

LADIES' BLOUSES.
Neat and Pretty Styles.
1/11 to 16/6
We hold a very large Selection of these goods in all the New Materials and Styles.

LARGE STOCK OF
Moreen, Cotton, and Silk Underskirts.

Ladies' Walking Skirts,
All Latest Styles and Trimmings.
4/11 to 25/-

Children's Sailor Costumes.
See page 6.

Ladies' Walking Skirts,
Washing Materials, 3/11 to 10/6

Goods sent on approval on receipt of Post or Country Order.

This late-nineteenth-century advertisement from Jacksons of Reading illustrates the growing variety of goods on offer and the increasing importance of fashion.

of different rooms with steps, passages and little 'nooks and crannies' — all of which added a sense of discovery and excitement to the shopping experience.

From the 1870s, some stores were doing so well that they were remodelled. Following its refurbishment in 1882, Arnott's of Glasgow boasted huge plate-glass windows, an attractive mosaic pavement and new counters. The introduction of plate glass in 1839 and the repeal of duties on glass in 1845 encouraged the widespread adoption of glass shop fronts — now considered a department store feature essential to the art of window-dressing. In 1884, the old frontage of Binns of Sunderland was replaced by a brick-and-stone façade with a central doorway paved with mosaic. Inside, many of the walls were removed to create a spacious open-plan showroom with mahogany counters. In 1893, the refurbished showrooms at D. H. Evans reopened with attractive oak fittings. Bainbridge's 'new grand showrooms', complete with new counters, display cabinets and lighting, opened in July 1898. A few stores had the good fortune — if one could call it that — of being destroyed by fire, thereby creating the need for a new purpose-built building. Such was the case with Whiteley's, which, following a devastating fire in 1887, was rebuilt as a five-storey block crowned with a central tower.

By the end of the nineteenth century, a new type of purpose-built store was emerging, often with an impressive exterior, large windows, spacious showrooms, attractive counters and cabinets, and lavish ornamentation. Mahogany or oak panelling, thick carpets, large mirrors and opulent light fittings were becoming the norm. Up-to-the-minute features such as electric lighting, escalators and sumptuous lifts were fitted, encouraging customers to explore every part of the store. At Glasgow's Colosseum store, for instance, three different types of electric lighting were installed in 1882. Retailers soon realised the marketing power of lighting their stores at night. Lewis's of Liverpool was one of the pioneers of night lighting: with

DEBENHAM & FREEBODY'S NEW PREMISES.
From a painting by Mortimer Menpes.

Described as 'rambling and inconvenient', the old Debenham & Freebody store was pulled down to make way for a gleaming new building, complete with lifts, restaurant, gentlemen's smoking rooms, and ladies' club room with adjoining dressing rooms. This artist's impression dates from 1907.

an electric light at the top of its tower, it stood out like a beacon in the Liverpool 'nightscape'.

Already in the 1830s, Dickens, in his *Sketches by Boz*, was commenting on the arrival of this new type of store:

> Six or eight years ago, the epidemic began to display itself among the linen drapers and haberdashers. The primary symptoms were an inordinate love of plate-glass and a passion for gas-light and gilding ... Quiet, dusty old shops in different parts of town were pulled down; spacious premises with stuccoed fronts and gold letters were erected instead. Floors were covered with Turkey carpets, roofs supported by massive pillars; doors knocked into windows; a dozen squares of glass into one; one shopman into a dozen ...

Department stores were quick to make use of advances in technology. The first known lift in Britain was installed at Glasgow's Wylie & Lochhead store in 1855. News of this amazing contraption was reported in the *Glasgow Herald*, which described it thus:

> ... a very ingenious hoisting apparatus, worked by a neat steam engine ... [in which] ... parties who are old, fat, feeble, short winded, or simple lazy, or who desire a bit of fun, have only to place themselves on an enclosed platform or flooring when they are elevated by a gentle and pleasing process to a height exceeding that of a country steeple.

In the 1880s, this type of steam-powered lift was superseded by the more efficient Otis lift, developed by the American Elisha Otis in 1852.

A 1910 photograph showing one of the rooms at Fenwick's in Newcastle. Ornate carved ceilings, plush carpets and sparkling chandeliers create a luxurious atmosphere designed to put customers in the mood to buy.

Two early Marshall & Snelgrove newspaper advertisements. Such simple adverts soon gave way to more elaborate designs.

MARSHALL & SNELGROVE.

BY ROYAL WARRANT

New Cloths & Tweeds

FOR THE

TAILOR-MADE GOWNS.

FASHIONABLE MILLINERY

FOR THE

EARLY SPRING.

Vere St. & Oxford St., W.

SUMMER FASHIONS.

MARSHALL & SNELGROVE.

BY ROYAL WARRANT

Ball, Fete and Evening Gowns.

Opera & Theatre Cloaks.

PARASOLS and EN TOUT CAS.

Vere St. & Oxford St., W.

PROVISION DEPARTMENT AT A
BIG STORES (HARROD'S).

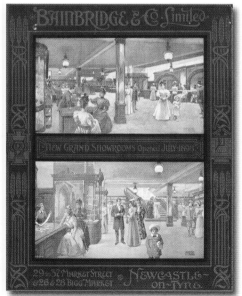

Above: Customers using the newly installed escalator at Harrods in 1901. Unlike our modern-day 'stepped' escalators, this one was simply a flat revolving belt.

This 1898 promotional blotter was designed to publicise the new showrooms at Bainbridge's. With shining glass cabinets, electric lighting, large counters and chairs for customers, it was the very latest in store comfort and design.

This 1904 postcard of Harrods shows just how impressive many of the larger department stores had become by the early twentieth century.

Le Bon Marché in Paris was famous for its colourful advertising campaigns. This free promotional card from the late nineteenth century shows a lady and her daughter selecting a doll from the toy department.

Above: Cash and payment slip are transported in a tube, such as this one, via a pipe from a sales desk to the central cash desk. A cashier then places the change and receipt in the tube, which then journeys back through the pipe to the appropriate sales desk.

Left: The still-functioning Lamson cash railway at Jacksons department store in Reading. The numbers on each pipe refer to the different departments.

In 1898, Harrods installed the first escalator ever to be seen in a British department store. Rather than featuring steps, the escalator consisted of a flat conveyor belt running upwards between the ground floor and first floor. On the day it was launched, shopmen stood at the top dispensing smelling salts and cognac to any customers frightened by the experience!

Another technical advance of the late nineteenth century to appear in department stores was the Lamson pneumatic tube system, or cash railway. Invented in the United States in the 1880s, this clever device featured dozens of numbered tubes, each one running from a department's sales desk to the central cash desk. When a customer made a purchase, the cash and sales slip were placed in a cash carrier and transported through a tube from the department to the cash desk. The cashier would then place the change and receipt in the carrier and pop it back in a tube connected to the relevant department. Cash was efficiently and safely transported around the store, with just one central and secure cash desk, thereby reducing security problems and theft.

By the end of the nineteenth century, department stores had become real 'palaces of commerce': sophisticated selling machines combining a whole range of devices – from advertising and promotions to sumptuous window displays and in-store entertainment – to seduce the customers into buying. The golden age of the department store had arrived.

WINTER SALE

at DERRY
& TOMS

KENSINGTON W. 8

LIFE AND SPECTACLE IN STORE

DESPITE two world wars and the Great Depression, the first half of the twentieth century was the golden age of the department store. Developments in window-dressing, advertising and retailing, combined with rapid changes in fashion, the emergence of new products and an ever-increasing spending power contributed to its success.

In the early twentieth century, window-dressing reached new artistic heights, becoming one of the primary means of attracting customers. A contemporary article in the *Drapers' Record* pointed out: 'Business is done less and less between the public and tradesmen and more and more between the public and the shop windows.' From about the 1890s new types of life-like wax figures began to replace the traditional armless and headless mannequins. In 1900 Arnott & Co. of Glasgow went perhaps a step too far by displaying mannequins with moving heads and eyes and heaving chests! A few stores – particularly Selfridges, which boasted twenty-one huge windows, all lit until midnight – created highly original themed displays or 'tableaux', specially designed to awe passers-by. One of these involved 8,000 sponges massed into one window, and another saw 'over 6,000 handkerchiefs exhaustively pinned, wired, folded and spread to fine geometric effect'. Some of the best displays involved weeks of preparation, such as Harrods' 1924 white sale window, which featured a 14-foot-high by 20-foot-long elephant made entirely of Terry towelling. At Lewis's in Liverpool, one particular window showed tweed outfits next to a lifelike representation of a crofter's cottage on the island of Harris (where the tweed originated). Other stores went for a more conservative approach, showcasing as many different products as possible. Whether treated as selling spaces or artful compositions, windows gradually became the specialist realm of the window-dresser.

Inside, stock was also elegantly displayed. Special stands – for hats, gloves, scarves and other items – added height and drama, and showed off each item to its best advantage. Furniture was shown in room settings; cutlery was laid out on tables as if ready for a meal; umbrellas were displayed fully open. By the 1920s, Barkers of Kensington featured forty 'specimen

Opposite: This 1919 poster for Derry & Toms department store is both simple and eye-catching and typical of the Art Deco era.

Selfridges became known for its arty, sometimes even outlandish, window displays. This one featured an assortment of sponges!

This 1922 photograph of Fenwick's (Newcastle) Cosmetic Hall illustrates just how much attention was given to the display and arrangement of items.

rooms' in which customers could find inspiration for furnishing their sitting room, kitchen, bedroom and bathroom.

With more stock shown within arm's reach, customers were encouraged to touch the articles for sale. An effective means of enticing people into buying, this new 'touchy-feely' approach also led to shoplifting, or

'kleptomania' as it was then described, and to counter this phenomenon many stores employed detectives. Shoplifting was generally committed by 'respectable' middle-class women; William Whiteley estimated that only one in every three hundred shoplifters caught in his store was a man. Contemporary journalists also reported a rise in so-called 'tabbies' – ladies who spent long periods of time in department stores enjoying the displays and facilities with no intention of ever buying anything.

'All Car Comforts greatly reduced' – Gamages took a full-page advert in *The Autocar* magazine to advertise its 1913 Spring Sale of motor clothing.

Selfridge Building, Oxford Street, London.

While the Selfridges store was being built a band of musicians was employed on site to speed up the building work!

In order to reach a wider market, stores started harnessing the power of advertising. At the end of the nineteenth century, a few stores had already seen the potential of taking advertising space in newspapers. Technical advances in printing during the nineteenth century – such as the development of presses capable of printing two sides of a page at once – meant that newspapers were much cheaper and enjoyed a greater circulation. Already in 1874 the Glasgow store Fraser & McLaren took an entire column on the front page of the *Glasgow Herald* to promote the opening of its new premises. By the early 1890s, Harrods had set up its own advertising department, making advertising history by taking a full page in the *Daily Telegraph* in 1894. Gamages was the first company to make the whole of the *Daily Mail* front page on 10 July 1904.

Perhaps the greatest advertising campaign of the early twentieth century was that of Selfridges, announcing its much-awaited opening in March 1909. During the entire week of its opening, Harry Gordon Selfridge commissioned thirty-eight advertisements designed by well-known graphic artists, appearing on over a hundred pages of eighteen national newspapers. The campaign, which cost £36,000 (equivalent to £2.35 million today), caused a sensation, with 90,000 people visiting the store on its opening day and over a million in the first week. The stylish adverts acted as open invitations with statements such as: 'Our invitation is to the whole of the British public and to visitors from overseas'. Interestingly, by this time

Harrods was already using an equally inclusive slogan on its own adverts: 'Harrods serves the world'.

Publicity – or the art of getting free editorial space in newspapers, magazines and other forms of media – often went hand in hand with conventional advertising. Harry Gordon Selfridge hired ex-journalist James Conaly as his press officer and even set up a special 'press club room', complete with typewriters, telephones and well-stocked bar, acting almost as a 'bait' for reporters. William Whiteley boasted that he never spent a penny on advertising, focusing all his efforts on publicity. His particular skill, blending showmanship with a nose for a good story, was in getting free editorials. Meanwhile, Selfridge became famous for his 'daily column', which he began publishing in 1912 under the pen name 'Callisthenes'. Almost 10,000 of these articles appeared between 1912 and the onset of the Second World War in 1939. Designed, of course, to promote Selfridges, they focused on topics such as the principles of good shopkeeping and the pleasures of shopping.

A 1930s advertisement for 'Gamages Famous Xmas Catalogue'. The box in the top-left-hand corner advertises the store's Christmas bazaar.

Some advertising campaigns inevitably focused on the summer and winter sales, the biggest events in the stores' calendar after Christmas. During the sales, which engendered a frenzy of excitement with customers queuing outside the stores for the 9 o'clock opening, bargain goods were piled together inviting customers to help themselves. Enterprising retailers saw the advantages of generating such 'sales-style' excitement at other times of the year. Within a few months of its opening in 1878, Bon Marché in Liverpool had launched its Christmas Fairyland, with themed displays, shows and grottoes. Similar 'Christmas bazaars' were soon taking place in most department stores across the country. Bentalls of Kingston staged an in-store circus during the Christmas period – including elephants and a lion, which were kept overnight in the lift shaft!

The Liverpool Bon Marché also featured more permanent attractions, including a model of Strasbourg Cathedral clock, which played music by Mozart, Rossini and Haydn each hour. The store also held flower shows and brass band concerts. Selfridges became particularly famous for its stunning shows and exhibits. When Frenchman Louis Blériot made aviation history on 25 July 1909 by flying over the Channel for the first time, Selfridge asked the pilot if he could 'borrow' the single-seat monoplane. For four days that week, the plane was seen by 150,000 people in the London store, which had to stay open until midnight to accommodate the crowds. In the 1920s, Selfridges installed an ice rink on its roof terrace where champion ice-skaters entertained the public and helped establish the trend for skating.

'A social centre, not a shop,' is the description Harry Gordon Selfridge gave of his Oxford Street store. This statement could equally well have described many of the other big department stores in the country, which were now popular meeting places. Bainbridge's promotional calendar of 1910 announced:

> We are pleased to find that many Ladies make our Warehouse a place of meeting in 'Town'. Of course the *spot of meeting* should always been named – The Blouse Room! The Millinery! The Flower and Perfume Gallery! The Ladies' Outfitting Room! The Tea Room – any other of the magnetic points in our Huge Emporium.

THE RENDEZVOUS AT MAULE'S, EDINBURGH

Certainly, the appearance of cloakrooms, tea rooms, reading rooms with free papers, writing rooms with free stationery and smoking rooms for men encouraged customers to linger. Such facilities also played a part in the emancipation of women at a time when there were very few places where a lady could have a meal on her own or see friends outside the home. It is slightly ironic, therefore, that the Suffragettes chose department stores as the focus of a window-smashing campaign in March 1912. While Barkers lost twenty windows, Harrods lost only two. As a gesture of support for the cause, Selfridges, which was also a target, decided to fly the Suffragette flag from its building rather than press charges.

Department stores were seen as convenient and relaxing meeting places, especially for out-of-town shoppers. In Edinburgh, Maule's opened an elegant restaurant called 'The Rendezvous', which soon became a fashionable gathering point. In the 1930s, Dickins & Jones's stunning Dome Restaurant, where tea dances were held every day, also became a popular rendezvous. A few stores enjoyed rooftop gardens – oases of tranquillity in busy town centres. Opened in May 1938, the Derry & Toms roof gardens comprised a sun pavilion and three different areas: an English woodland garden, a Spanish garden and a Tudor garden. Now known as Kensington Roof Gardens, they are something of a surprise on busy Kensington High Street and well worth a visit.

The biggest department stores included an almost unimaginable number of 'leisure' facilities and services. By 1909, Harrods boasted:

Most department stores had a fleet of delivery vans. This photograph dates from 1910.

> ... elegant and restful waiting and retiring rooms for both sexes, writing rooms with dainty stationery, club room, fitting rooms, smoking rooms, a post office, theatre ticket office, railway and steamer ticket and tourist office, appointment board where one can leave notes for friends, a circulating library and music room.

One service that almost every department store offered from the outset was home delivery. At first, horse-drawn carts were used, but these were gradually replaced by motor vans. In 1906 Harrods was using 410 horses, 10 motor vans, 157 despatch vans and 52 removal vans, and was offering free delivery for any item throughout England and Wales. Painted in their own 'store colours' and travelling the length and breadth of Britain, department store vans were a powerful form of free advertising. Their use was also boosted by the advent of mail order, which sometimes represented about a third of a store's turnover. Already in the late nineteenth century Harrods was printing a 1,000-page illustrated catalogue, described as 'a veritable shopping encyclopaedia ... handsomely bound in cloth, lettered in gold and ... worthy of a place in the domestic library.' Some of these catalogues, with attractive full-colour cover designs, are now collectable items.

As stores grew in size, departments became almost independent operating units with their own managers and buyers. Sales staff who until now had 'lived in' – often in grim top-floor dormitories or nearby hostels – were increasingly free to choose their own accommodation. One of the last to make the transition was the Peter Robinson store, where, until the First World War, employees lived in conditions described as 'a blend of semi-monastic institution and the fairly strict boarding school'. The gruelling 12 hour days became shorter, prompted by a 1909 bill prohibiting shop workers from working more than 60 hours a week and enforcing early closing one day a week. Gradually, too, the highly unfair system of staff fines – for anything from being late to missing a sale – was removed. Some stores pioneered forms of staff benefits, such as staff discount schemes, free training and at least one week's holiday per year. Debenham & Freebody had its own education department and held three evening classes per week for young assistants. Selfridges held compulsory morning staff training sessions for the entire workforce. By the First World War, many large stores retained the services of a doctor for staff; some even had visiting dentists.

Department store staff were tested to the limit during the First World War. When war was declared on 4 August 1914, male workers, especially van drivers, were enlisted at once. The delivery fleet at Howells in Cardiff was requisitioned by the War Office, while at Dickins & Jones the Government commandeered the

'An ideal blouse for war workers,' states this 1916 advertisement. Simple yet elegant, this shirt is typical of women's clothing during the First World War.

PRACTICAL BLOUSES FOR WOMEN WORKERS

Designed to meet the present demand for becoming blouses that can be guaranteed to stand hard wear.

STRONG SILK BLOUSE, as sketch, in rich Satin Merveilleux, made in our own workrooms, full ample shape, finished with lace collar. An ideal blouse for war workers. In a very large range of practical colours to wear with tweed skirts, also in vivid shades to wear with navy skirts, including black and navy. Stocked in four sizes.

SPECIAL PRICE
15/9

Also in blue and white spot Foulards and practical Shirtings or in good white linen at the same price.
Sent on Approval.
Catalogue Post Free.

Debenham & Freebody
Wigmore Street.
(Cavendish Square) London. W.

store's horses. Dickins & Jones paid a retaining wage and sent Christmas food parcels to all staff who fought in the war, as well as guaranteeing them a job on their return. Some stores also offered discounts on products and the free use of their premises to war-work charities. Selfridges gave free afternoon teas to 'sewing circles', and its Palm Court Orchestra played 'Rule Britannia'. And, despite restricted supplies and ever-increasing casualties, a 'sense of fashion was kept alive'. The trend was towards simpler, practical clothes that could be easily mass-produced. To save on fabric, women's skirts became shorter and blouses more close fitting.

Despite the horrors of this 'war to end all wars', many historians have argued that the years that followed were a period of economic boom and dramatically improved living conditions for the lower classes of society. It is perhaps not surprising, therefore, to find that the large department stores increased their share of the total retail trade from between 1.5 per cent and 3 per cent in 1910 to between 3 and 4 per cent in 1920. By the 1920s they accounted for about 10 per cent of national sales of furniture and furnishings, boosted by a rise in the number of home owners. Privately owned houses and newly built council properties were smaller than before, creating a new market for compact and less ostentatious furnishings.

Cheap, ready-to-wear clothes became the norm and made for increased sales, as women, many of whom were now working and had money in their pockets, were happy to change their wardrobes more often. The growing desire to be fashionable was boosted by the stars of the popular 'talking films' shown in new cinemas up and down the country. A new craze for sport and bathing, helped by an increase in the amount of leisure and holiday time, also opened up new markets. Holidays became a national habit for both rich and poor, with the number of workers

This early 1920s John Lewis advertisement displays the fashion typical of this era, including knee-length skirts and cloche hats.

John Lewis & Co.

STANMORE. This is a tailored Costume. The coat is double-breasted and the skirt has a deep pleat on each side. In fine quality suiting and lined with crêpe de Chine. Sizes : S.W. and W.   4 Gns. O.S. 7/6 extra.

LYNTON. A plain tailored Costume, with single-breasted coat. The skirt has three pleats at the side to allow freedom of movement. In navy and black : in colours to order. Lined with crêpe de Chine. Sizes S.W. and W. O.S. 7/6 extra.   6 Gns.

BOSTON. A trim little Suit with a half-belted coat, equally appropriate for country or town wear, and lined with crêpe de Chine. Sizes : Petite, S.W., and W.   4½ Gns.

Swan & Edgar LTD

SALE

Begins on Mon., Jan. 4th

Complete Fashion ranges and entire collections of the latest Accessories—all drastically reduced in price.

"Amber." An Evening Two-piece. Satin low-backed dress and new tail coat of poult. Royal blue dress/red coat, royal blue/self, imperial red/self, gold/brown, gold/royal, sky/self, black/self. Hip sizes : 38, 40, 42 and 44ins.

Sale price **40/-**

"Tricolour." A new Tunic Evening Gown in smart patterned prints. In lovely designs on pastel and dark grounds. Hip sizes : 38, 40, 42 and 44ins.
Sale price **50/-**

Inexpensive Frocks : Second Floor

This cover from Swan & Edgar's 1937 Winter Sale booklet highlights the fashion for glamorous evening dresses.

entitled to a paid holiday rising from 1.5 million in the 1920s to 11 million in 1939.

New car owners were catered for in many of the larger stores, which were obviously keen to latch on to this lucrative new market. Car-related accessories, such as fur-lined over-boots or specially designed 'motor trunks', appeared in top-end stores, including Harrods. Howells in Cardiff went as far as opening its own motor showroom in 1924. Electrical goods, too, were an emerging market. In November 1922, the BBC made its first radio broadcast,

A 1930s John Lewis shop window displaying beachwear and lingerie.

heralding a new age of mass-produced wireless sets. Selfridges, always at the forefront of all things technical, launched the first ever television department with a major in-store exhibition in 1939.

This 1935 bicycle advertisement was one of many promoting sport-related items during the inter-war years.

Efficient Luggage for Easter Jaunts

BOLSTER BAG (on left)

Light, capacious and conveniently fitted with 'lightning' fastener. In good quality grained hide, leather lined.

Size 18 ins. 55/-   20 ins. 60/-   22 ins. 65/-
Size 24 ins. 70/-   26 ins. 75/-   28 ins. 81/-

Trunks,
First Floor

MOTOR TRUNK (on right)

A practical trunk of new design, with domed top, strongly made of three-ply, lined and covered with Rexine. Water-tight and dust-proof, it contains two full-size black suit cases and is fitted with lever clips and dust-proof locks.

30×17½×16 ins. £7 7 0
33×17½×16 ins. £8 2 6
36×17½×16 ins. £8 15 0

Three-ply Trunk, covered in strong leather-cloth, with fibre binding.
30×17½×16 ins. £5 5 0

HARRODS LTD   **HARRODS**   LONDON SW1

A 1929 Harrods advertisement promoting 'Efficient Luggage for Easter Jaunts'. It features a wonderful 'water-tight and dust-proof' motor trunk.

This 1926 Peter Jones advertisement illustrates the emergence of the electrical goods market.

Developments in retailing saw the rise of branded products, whose prices were increasingly fixed by manufacturers. This development removed an important freedom from the stores, which had long been used to setting their own prices in line with specific promotions and sales, or in response to their own market. A few stores responded to this threat by creating their own brands. Lewis's of Liverpool introduced the Standex and Wilwer labels. Barkers sold a range of items under the Kenbar brand. Harrods was particularly successful, banking on its exclusive image to sell (as it still does) many own-brand products.

Another threat came from the proliferation of chain and co-operative stores, such as W. H. Smith, Woolworth's, Marks & Spencer and the Army & Navy. Their major advantage was their ability to buy centrally, which enabled them to achieve better deals from their suppliers, at a time when most department stores were still independent concerns. But all this was about to change. Lewis's, with shops in Liverpool, Manchester, Sheffield and Birmingham, was the first department store to introduce a central buying policy. In 1923, it opened a Central

AN ELECTRIC DISTURBANCE.

Pray do not imagine that the unsteady appearance of this group is intended to symbolise the "After-Christmas-Dinner" state of mind. To tell the truth the photographer became so much elated by the prospect of the wireless set in the centre, that he rose above his subject.

FOR PRICES SEE BACK.

Peter Jones
Sloane Square

Although Tudor in style, the Liberty store was actually built in the 1920s. The oak and teak used in the building were taken from two ships, HMS *Impregnable* and HMS *Hindustan*.

This 1920s photograph shows the palatial proportions of Lewis's in Liverpool. It was one of many department stores to be targeted during the Second World War.

Buying Office in London, employing forty buyers.

During this period, successful stores also started 'buying up' other stores. Harrods, which had already acquired Dickins & Jones in 1914, took over Kendal Milne in 1919, Swan & Edgar in 1920, D. H. Evans in 1928 and Schoolbred's in 1931. In 1919, Debenhams took over Marshall's and started negotiating the purchase of Harvey Nichols. In South Kensington, Barkers acquired Pontings in 1907, and Derry & Toms in 1920. Binns of Sunderland gradually acquired regional stores and built up a chain of small department stores on the north-east coast and in southern Scotland.

Lewis's, Liverpool

During the 1920s, Selfridges bought a total of nineteen stores in London, Dublin, Liverpool, Leeds, Sheffield, Peterborough, Northampton, Gloucester, Windsor, Watford and Brighton. Established in 1926, Selfridge Provincial Stores consisted of Bon Marché in Brixton, Quin & Axten of Brixton, Holdrons of Peckham, Barrats of Clapham and Pratts of Streatham. Selfridges' most illustrious take-over was that of Whiteley's in 1927.

As during the First World War, staff and parts of department store buildings were requisitioned in the Second World War. Harrods' fashion workrooms were put to good use for the making of uniforms, while parachutes and even aircraft parts were manufactured on the premises. At Howells in Cardiff, rooms were adapted for the production of uniforms and parachutes, and the garage used for war-related repair work. Here, as elsewhere, about a quarter of the staff enlisted, requiring the store to depend more heavily on women workers.

Located mainly in city centres, department stores were prime targets during air raids. In September 1940, John Lewis on Oxford Street suffered £2 million of bomb damage. Lewis's store in Liverpool suffered a blow on the night of 3 May 1941, with most of the building destroyed. The parts of the building that survived intact were quickly adapted and reopened for business by the end of May. Binns in Sunderland was damaged by bombing in 1941. Throughout the country, shops began to close at five o'clock to allow staff time to get home before the raids started. During the winter months, West End stores were forced to send staff home before night set in at about four o'clock.

At the Barker group of stores, over sixty men and women acted as fire-watchers every night. In the daytime, hundreds of workers were ready to act as air-raid wardens, firemen and first-aid squads. At the first sign of an air raid, the store was immediately closed and customers inside were escorted to the safety of the basements, which had been transformed into bomb-proof air-raid shelters. Staff working on first-aid and fire-fighting teams promptly changed into their uniforms and assumed their new roles, while the company vans became ambulances. Meanwhile, nurses were available to help the injured. With their large, multi-talented teams of people and efficient management systems, the big department stores were particularly efficient at putting in place such security measures.

Even during the war, a sense of fashion was kept alive, as this Whiteley's booklet demonstrates.

37

This 1941 photograph shows hosiery assistants (left to right) Mary Irvine, Alice McGregor, Mary Craik and Lily Coles at McEwens in Perth.

Staff at Oxford Street's John Lewis inspecting damage after the September 1940 bombing.

On 1 June 1941 rationing of clothing and footwear began. Everyone was issued with a limited number of coupons for the next year. There were set numbers of coupons required for every item: 'nine for an unlined mackintosh

Harrods female employees in wartime uniforms. Each woman works for a different service (left to right): the Land Army, Voluntary Services, St John Ambulance Brigade, Royal Emergency Naval Service, Red Cross, Auxiliary Territorial Service, Civil Nursing Reserve, Auxiliary Air Force and the Mechanised Transport Corps.

A 1944–5 clothing book. Rationing continued until well after the end of the war, finally ending in 1953.

or cape; eleven for a dress, gown or frock; six for a night-dress ...' Some of the more useful or essential articles were exempt, including boilersuits, knickers and shorts. In late 1941 the Utility scheme was introduced. Covering clothes, shoes and furniture, it was designed to produce cheap, standardised items. Restrictions – from the amount of fabric used to the number of buttons on an item – were introduced to save on materials. Clothes were marked with the CC41 symbol, which stood for 'Civilian Clothing 1941'. Unfortunately the scheme involved confusing regulations, which added to the pressures on shop staff. Undeterred and keen to remain optimistic, Bon Marché in Liverpool staged a fashion show featuring the new Utility styles! As we will see in the next section, clothes rationing was to continue beyond the end of the war.

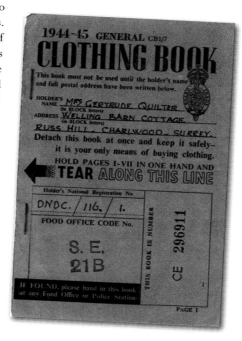

1944-45 GENERAL CB1/7
CLOTHING BOOK
This book must not be used until the holder's name and full postal address have been written below.

HOLDER'S NAME *Mrs Gertrude Quilter* (in BLOCK letters)
ADDRESS *Welling Barn Cottage* (in BLOCK letters)
Russ Hill - Charlwood - Surrey.
Detach this book at once and keep it safely— it is your only means of buying clothing.
HOLD PAGES 1-VII IN ONE HAND AND
TEAR ALONG THIS LINE

Holder's National Registration No.
DNDC. / 116. / 1.
FOOD OFFICE CODE No.
S. E.
21B

THIS BOOK IS NUMBER
CE 296911

IF FOUND, please hand in this book at any Food Office or Police Station.
PAGE 1

THE POST-WAR ERA

O NE of the most significant social and economic impacts of the Second World War was the rise in earnings and subsequent change in status of the working class, which in 1945 constituted about 60 per cent of the population. Staff shortages during and after the war meant that workers were able to ask for higher wages. Between 1951 and 1961, the weekly earnings of men aged over twenty-one almost doubled from £8.30 to £15.35 – a much higher increase than the rate of inflation at the time.

Department stores soon began to notice the changing nature of their customer base. As early as the 1940s, the luxury store Brown's of Chester was employing a team of experts to research ways in which it could make its store more attractive to working-class customers. In a report dated 1953, the International Association of Department Stores recorded problems in Britain's top-of-the-range stores. Two years later, it was advising its British members to focus on the 'prosperous council house tenant'. Harrods was one of the first stores to respond to changes in the market. In 1953 it acquired stores in Birmingham, Manchester and Sheffield – cities with a high proportion of skilled workers.

One of the first measures stores took to attract working-class customers was to do away with large 'intimidating' counters and to introduce self-service. Whiteley's, Beales of Bournemouth, Debenhams and many other stores quickly made the transition. Others opted for self-service areas, such as Lewis's in Liverpool, which in May 1952 installed a self-service fashion shop in its store.

As stores became more sophisticated in their marketing, they began to realise the importance of developing an identity in line with their own particular market. The three Kensington stores of Pontings, Barkers and Derry & Toms are a striking example of this idea. During the 1950s, they became famous for their three grades of trading, from the popular Pontings, through the medium-priced Barkers to the exclusive Derry & Toms. Not surprisingly, Pontings adopted the slogans 'The House for Value' and 'Value in Store', while Derry & Toms described itself as 'a beautiful store to sell beautiful things'. By this time, the three stores had become famous for their

Opposite:
This beautifully lit 1950s fashion photograph shows a smartly dressed model descending one of the escalators at Harrods.

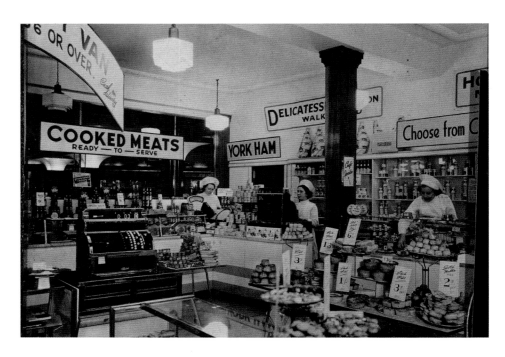

An early 1950s photograph of the delicatessen section at Fenwick's in Newcastle. Note the two enormous cash registers.

'Sales Specials' – specially organised train journeys for out-of-town customers timed to coincide with the sales. Waves of bargain-hunters would swarm up from the adjacent High Street Kensington underground station, flooding the stores.

Gradually, some stores started attracting a range of different customers by creating 'shops within a shop'. House of Fraser introduced 'Junior Miss' sections in some of their stores as a means of getting more business from young women. Similarly, in 1947, Dickins & Jones launched a 'Young Londoner' department, in a bid to attract a younger clientele.

These developments coincided with a new cult of youth and an ever-increasing passion for fashion. In 1947, the French couturier Christian Dior unveiled his 'New Look'. Emphasising the female figure, with fitted bodices, cinched waists and full skirts, New Look outfits soon appeared in every department store in the country. This opulent style came to symbolise the start of a new optimistic era after the ravages of war. However, up until the 1950s some women couldn't afford ready-made New Look clothes (and the Utility clothing scheme was in fact not wound up until 1952). Instead, customers went for the cheaper home-dressmaking option and selected suitable patterns from the many in-store pattern departments and material from associated fabric departments.

Ballet length dress of shimmer striped nylon sheer for summer evenings.

FREDERICK STARKE designed it.

AT McDONALD'S LTD. 31 BUCHANAN STREET GLASGOW · · · JAMES STREET

This 1953 advertisement illustrates the contemporary fashion for New Look dresses, with their tight waists and ample skirts. At the time fashion was heavily influenced by Hollywood; it's no surprise that the model looks like Grace Kelly.

Even relatively small department stores, such as Trewin Brothers in Watford, adopted the New Look style.

SPRING AND SUMMER FROCKS

1953

SHELLY

TREWIN BROTHERS
QUEENS ROAD
WATFORD
Telephone: Watford 7081

Tapping into the younger market was also a means of counteracting the threats posed by the emerging fashion boutiques. Mary Quant and her future husband Alexander Plunkett-Greene started the trend when they opened their boutique, Bazaar, on the King's Road in 1955. Reacting against the mass appeal and large-scale advertising of department and chain stores, small independent clothes shops started appearing across the country in the late 1950s and 1960s.

Partly in response to the threat of emerging boutiques, Harrods opened its revolutionary 'Way In' boutique in 1967, which is still open today. Astonished by the event,

An early 1950s
fashion show at
the John Lewis
Welwyn store.

The bustling fabric
department at
Oxford Street's
John Lewis store in
1966.

the *Drapers' Record* reported: 'Traditional retailers with a lifetime of in-built concepts about how to serve the customer will never have seen anything like it.' The 'Way In' concept turned the idea of separate departments on its head: for the first time, women's and men's clothing were shown in the same area, together with other related items. As Fraser's chairman Hugh Fraser explained:

> Goods were grouped according to the activities they serve – thus sea and seaside needs might be served by a 'beach boutique' selling clothes, boats, picnic and camping kit and sporting gear, so saving customers from trailing round several departments.

For the first time, too, displays were planned to be low maintenance and low cost, relying on modular and lighter units, reflecting contemporary furniture styles.

Although many department stores found it hard to reflect the liberal attitudes and dress of the Swinging Sixties, some tried to keep up with the times. In 1964, Barkers staged a 'Youthquake' event during which models danced along the catwalk to pop music, flaunting clothes by Britain's 'new young designers'. Meanwhile, a host of stores went down the 'boutique' route.

An early 1970s photograph of the ladies' fashion department in the John Lewis Welwyn store. Note how related items – such as hats, sun cream, chairs, parasol and beachwear – are all being sold and displayed in one area.

This Liberty advertisement illustrates the 1950s fashion for light, portable furniture with typically tapered legs.

Liberty

Liberty's live up to their reputation for matchless quality and design with their contemporary collection of price-controlled English, Scottish and Scandinavian furniture . . . Swedish glass . . . modern light fittings . . . and their own Liberty-designed occasional pieces and hand-printed furnishing fabrics.

of Regent Street

In 1966, Selfridges opened its first Miss Selfridge shop, aimed at girls between the ages of 17 and 22. In the 1970s and 1980s, the Fraser group of stores started opening popular 'Lifestyle' departments, in which clothes, furnishings and other items representing one image were displayed. Their slogan was: 'It's what you wear. It's how you live.'

The 'shop-within-a-shop' concept gradually turned into what is now called – in retailing terminology – a 'concentration', where goods from one brand or manufacturer are displayed in one area. The idea was first introduced in 1978 in Kendal Milne's revamped first-floor fashion department named 'Collections'. The floor featured 11 'concentrations' of

Out of the blue...

Ballantyne at Deben[...]

Cloud-soft . . . feather-light Cashmeres in a symphony of [...]

This 1959 advertisement is an example of brand-focused advertising. Debenhams is using the Ballantyne brand to promote its store.

An early 1980s Miss Selfridge advertisement. Launched in the 1960s, Miss Selfridge stores soon became popular with young women; early mannequins were based on the fashion icon Twiggy.

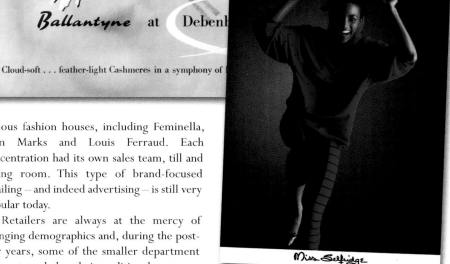

Miss Selfridge

famous fashion houses, including Feminella, John Marks and Louis Ferraud. Each concentration had its own sales team, till and fitting room. This type of brand-focused retailing – and indeed advertising – is still very popular today.

Retailers are always at the mercy of changing demographics and, during the post-war years, some of the smaller department stores struggled as their traditional customer

base moved to different areas. Some stores ceased trading, such as Brixton's Bon Marché and Brown's of Workington. Meanwhile, other more successful stores underwent major refurbishments or were completely rebuilt – sometimes as a consequence of war damage. During the 1950s, the Howells store in Cardiff was revamped with new open-plan sales floors. In 1957, the new Middlesbrough Binns store opened, featuring six open-plan floors and an elegant elliptical staircase. Walsh's in Sheffield opened its new store in 1953, featuring all the latest technology, including air conditioning and modern lighting systems. Many other stores took advantage of technical developments, doing away with their 'old-fashioned' dark wood fittings, opting instead for glass counters and lighter – and often much cheaper – furniture. One of the biggest department

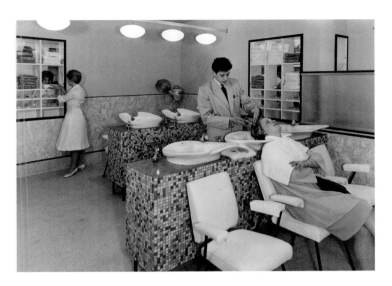

A late 1960s photograph of the hairdressing department at John Lewis on Oxford Street.

stores to be rebuilt in the 1950s was Oxford Street's John Lewis. In 1962, Barbara Hepworth's striking sculpture, *Winged Figure*, was added to one side

The escalators at Oxford Street's John Lewis, c. 1960.

The electrical department at Bonds in Norwich in 1983.

of the building. Today the store's exterior stands as an impressive reminder of a lost era.

Technological developments led to the appearance of new products, which in turn gave rise to new types of departments. These focused mainly on electrical goods for the home, such as radio and television sets, refrigerators and vacuum cleaners, which became increasingly affordable in the second half of the twentieth century. Televisions were still a rare possession in the early 1950s, but by 1971, 90 per cent of all households owned one. As well as offering new, up-to-date products, many of the larger department stores continued to be popular for their range of services and their role as a meeting place. A survey in the late 1970s stated that 47 per

A young girl being fitted for her new school uniform at Oxford Street's John Lewis in 1968.

cent of British women (and 20 per cent of all adults) visited a department store at least once a month.

As with all commercial ventures, takeovers are at times inevitable. There are far too many to list in this book and one would need a whole chapter to discuss the subject in detail, but it seems important to note two major takeovers of the immediate post-war years. In 1951 the Lewis's Group bought Selfridges and in 1957 Harrods was acquired by House of Fraser. Over the course of the next fifty years, takeovers almost became the norm, with some stores changing hands a number of times. Selfridges, for instance, was taken over by the Sears Group in 1965 and was bought in 2003 by the Canadian businessman Galen Weston. Harrods was bought by the Al-Fayed family in 1985. At the same time, many independent stores became part of a larger 'family' of stores, including House of Fraser, Debenhams, Fenwick's and John Lewis.

The rise in carownership from the 1960s led to major changes in the 'geography of retailing'. Seeing a new potential market in attractive and historic towns, which carowners were increasingly visiting as a day out, Fenwick's opened stores in Canterbury, Tunbridge Wells, York and Windsor. Thanks partly to this cunning move, by the late 1980s Fenwick's was one of the most successful British department store groups. In the 1970s, the Brent Cross shopping centre became one of the first successful 'out-of-town' shopping centres. Many retailing experts have claimed that its success was due mainly to its two 'anchor tenants', Fenwick's and John Lewis. Linked to specially designed car

This 1950s advertisement invites 'weary shoppers' to take a break at Fenwick's restaurant and tea room.

This satirical cartoon by Frank Boyle appeared in the Scottish press when it was announced in March 2005 that Jenners had been bought by House of Fraser.

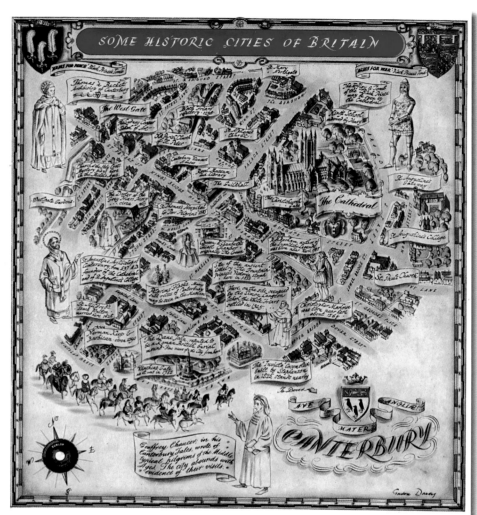

To walk through Canterbury is to see, written in stone, the proud story of England's greatness. Priest and prelate, baron and burgess, prince and peasant, all have lived their hour and left memorial behind them in church and palace and cottage of this treasured city. Through its streets have passed the centuries-long procession of pilgrims to the shrine of the martyred Becket. To-day, though the busy life of a machine age laps its walls, it is still, in its brooding greatness, the shrine of beauty and of peace.

ONE OF A SERIES OF DECORATIVE PLANS SPECIALLY DRAWN FOR THE DUNLOP RUBBER COMPANY LIMITED

parks, inner-city shopping centres also became a magnet for big-name department stores. Officially opened in 1976, Eldon Square in Newcastle was one of the very first. It housed both John Lewis and Fenwick's stores.

While many stores focused on establishing a presence in such 'mall-type' premises, a few worked on restoring the beauty of their original, and often palatial, buildings while at the same time modernising and extending their selling space. In 1987 Harrods announced that it was to spend £200 million over five years to re-create the original splendour of the store. The aim was to transform Harrods into a 'palace of romance, fantasy and history'. The budget included £15 million for new marble floors and carpets and the plan involved the creation of 40,000 square feet of new selling space. Many other London stores gradually followed this example.

Such luxurious revamps were part of a general trend that saw department stores 'trading up'. While they had been keen to tap into the lower end of the market after the Second World War, in the 1980s stores started to disassociate themselves from cut-price retailers, aiming instead for the upper end of the market. Department stores had come full circle.

Opposite:
This 1950s Dunlop advertisement is one of a series showing historic British cities, whose visitor numbers increased as a result of the rise in car ownership from the 1950s onwards. Keen to benefit from this influx, Fenwick's established successful stores at Canterbury, York and Windsor in the 1980s.

A window display at Oxford Street's John Lewis in 1979.

TODAY'S STORE

THE RECENT PAST has seen a number of impressive department store refurbishments. Between 1999 and 2004, the iconic 1930s Peter Jones store in Chelsea was given an overhaul by architects John McAslan and Partners. The store stayed open throughout its £107 million refurbishment, although some departments were moved from the main shop to its nearby warehouse, which served as a temporary selling area. The revamp included a new high-tech air-cooling system, new restaurants, the repositioning of escalators in a stunning central atrium and a 20 per cent increase in sales space. The John Lewis store on Oxford Street underwent a similar refurbishment in 2007. Costing over £60 million, the project turned the store into a more unified space with two splendid glass-roofed atriums, a new restaurant and an impressive new food hall — including a whole room dedicated to cheese!

Since 2004 and under the direction of Alannah Weston, daughter of the store's owner Galen Weston, Selfridges is gradually returning to its Art Deco glamour. As creative director, Alannah has organised a number of in-store art exhibitions and traffic-stopping window displays, one of which featured a model stripping naked as part of a fragrance promotion. She has also overseen the creation of stunning new in-store boutiques, of which the Wonder Room is perhaps the most successful. This elegant new space, which has been described as a 'luxury cabinet of curiosities', aims to bring back an element of surprise and awe into the shopping experience. Items for sale range from black-diamond jewellery pieces to ostrich-leather bags.

It is not only the big London stores that have been investing in their buildings. As a result of the acquisition of neighbouring premises, the family-run Banburys store in Barnstaple, Devon, was rebuilt and expanded in the early 1980s. In 2005, the store was extended by a further 50 per cent. In 1989 the company bought the large and old-fashioned Eastmond & Co. store in Tiverton. It was promptly refurbished.

A similar tale can be told for McEwens of Perth, Scotland's largest independent retailer. In 1997, when a nearby property became available,

Opposite:
After John Lewis, Debenhams is the second-biggest 'anchor store' in the new Liverpool One, a shopping, leisure and residential centre in Liverpool.

The Wonder Room at Selfridges has been described as a 'luxury gifts emporium with the energy of a souk'.

Graceful 'space-age' escalators in the central atrium at Peter Jones in London.

Staff at McEwens of Perth celebrating the store's 140th anniversary in 2008.

sales space was expanded to include a new homewares section. The latter was so popular that the company moved the department, renamed 'McEwens at Home', into two large warehouses in 2000. In the same year, McEwens also bought a new store in Inverness. In 2008 McEwens opened a 'Boutique' – a mix of independently designed fashion, shoes, accessories and objects for the home – and celebrated its 140th anniversary.

Even more recently, Boswells, the much-loved family-owned department store in Oxford, has been re-branded with a fresh new logo, and partly refitted with a new linens department and new staircase. Camp Hopson of Newbury, also family-owned, underwent major refurbishments in the 1990s and in the early part of the twenty-first century.

It is clear that big-name stores occupy a large part of the market. In 2008, House of Fraser had 63 stores across the UK and Ireland; Debenhams about 150 in the UK, Republic of Ireland and Northern Ireland; and the John Lewis Partnership 27 in England and Scotland. In 2007, John Lewis was voted Britain's Favourite Department Store. Unlike many other well-known stores, it has focused on selling home and electrical items, rather than devoting more and more sales space to clothes. It is also unique in its business model: each member of staff is a partner, and therefore has a stake, in the business.

Some independents have of course ceased trading, including the much-loved Blacklers store in Liverpool, which closed in 1988, exactly a hundred years after it first opened. Its famous rocking horse, Blackie, which gave rides to generations of Liverpool children, now resides at the Museum of Liverpool Life. A major closure of the recent past was that of the Allders chain in 2005 when all of its forty-five stores were closed and over 1,000 jobs were lost.

A few independents are bucking the trend, thanks in part to their membership of the Associated Independent Stores (AIS) organisation. As its website explains: 'AIS enables independent department stores and specialist retailers to profit from the level of buying power and services normally enjoyed by big high street chains – yet with no loss of their independence.' Many of these independent stores are still family-owned, such as Hancock & Wood of Warrington, Austins of Newton Abbot, Jacksons of Reading and Roomes of Upminster. Many are proud of being independent and of their ability to offer a unique, sometimes even quirky, shopping experience. With its 1960s wood fittings, Jacksons of Reading was once lovingly described as 'the timewarp department store'. It takes you back to a time when the customer was king. As its website proudly states: 'We still serve our customer. It is not self-service here and to us each customer is a VIP.' When you make a purchase, your money goes through the Lamson tube to the central cashier, and your change and hand-written receipt are sent back in a little tube. Should you ever want your initials put on your top hat, simply ask one of the helpful menswear staff: tucked away in a corner is a box filled with metal hat initials. With its impressive food hall that wouldn't look out of place in a London store, Bakers & Larners of Holt is equally charming. As at Jacksons, each department has its own sales staff and counter. Many of these independent stores have developed the knack of selling items that you just wouldn't find anywhere else.

Nowadays, perhaps more so than ever before, department stores come in all shapes and sizes and offer a plethora of experiences. There are those where time has stood still. Here is your chance to revel in a bit of nostalgia: as you go through the door, you step back in time. Then there are those stores that have been restored, revealing their building's original beauty while also keeping up with the times with modern fixtures and fittings. And, finally, there are those that are completely new, with almost space-age interiors. The most obvious example of this last type of store is the Selfridges building in Birmingham. Completed in 2003 and designed by avant-garde architects Future Systems – best known for their award-winning media centre at Lord's Cricket Ground – this curvaceous building is unlike any other department store. As the architects explain:

Jacksons of Reading is the ultimate shopping experience for all nostalgia junkies. Here you can still get your hat cleaned with a special hat brush and your initials pinned onto it.

Our brief was not only to design a state-of-the-art department store but also to create an architectural landmark for Birmingham so that the building itself would become a genuine catalyst for urban regeneration. The skin is made up of thousands of aluminium discs, creating a fine, lustrous grain like the scales of a snake or the sequins of a Paco Rabanne dress.

Birmingham's Selfridges building defies all stylistic categorisation; it acts as a magnet in the city's highly popular Bullring Shopping Centre.

The building has become a Birmingham icon and, for some, it is reason enough to visit the city. Another new landmark store is the £44 million John Lewis store in Leicester, which opened in 2008. The elegant swirling pattern on its glass wall was inspired by a nineteenth-century block-print design and harks back to Leicester's important textile heritage. At night, the wall is lit from within, creating a shimmering, almost jewel-like effect. Such stores offer a sense of theatre and excitement in much the same way as their Victorian and Edwardian predecessors did over a hundred years ago.

Successful retailers know that shopping is about more than just products; it is about the whole 'shopping experience'. This is perhaps why department stores – with their various departments, their restaurants and services – have stood the test of time and why some have, it seems, enjoyed a new lease of life in recent years. According to Verdict Research, the department store sector returned to growth in 2006 after a number of years of decline. Paul Kelly, Selfridges' chief executive, told the *Daily Telegraph* in January 2008:

A stylish '1960s retro' café at a Debenhams store.

'For years people have been writing department stores off.' But things are looking bright for Selfridges, whose profits increased by 33 per cent in the year to 31 January 2007. Like many other department stores, House of Fraser and John Lewis have experienced a boost thanks to their comprehensive and easy-to-use websites – acting as online catalogues, but also as one of the most powerful and important marketing tools for any twenty-first-century business. Successful store websites are, indeed, more than mere catalogues;

they work as virtual shop windows aimed at enticing customers into their buildings.

Beyond an investment in their structures, stores have continued to focus on brands and events as important promotional tools. A key success for Debenhams was its introduction in the 1990s of the 'Designers at Debenhams' concept, combining the talents of Jasper Conran, John Richmond and John Rocha among others. Since then, the store has continued its policy of designer- and celebrity-led retailing. Liberty, meanwhile, recently launched a collection of fabrics designed by established British artists, including Turner Prize winner Grayson Perry.

As was the case a hundred years ago, Selfridges is still a cut above the rest when it comes to PR campaigns. In 2009, in celebration of its 100th anniversary, it held a star-studded anniversary party, a fascinating exhibition (whose beautiful and inventive displays would make most museum curators envious), as well as many anniversary-related displays and events. The store even went as far as exhibiting a replica of the Blériot plane, in memory of their crowd-pulling 1909 display.

In a similar bid to act as places of instruction and entertainment, John Lewis stores also offer a varied programme of events, from celebrity book signings to in-store knitting workshops. During the summer holidays, some John Lewis stores host children's activities, including magic shows, face painting, biscuit decorating and teddy bears' picnics. In 2009, Liberty recently re-launched its 'sewing school', with a range of sewing and knitting demonstrations.

Selfridges' 100th anniversary magazine.

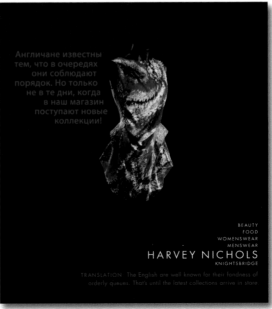

One of the humorous advertisements in Harvey Nichols' 2009 'tourist ad campaign'.

Even when closed, a department store can be a beautiful sight. This is the Harvey Nichols store in Edinburgh.

As always, ingenious and targeted advertising also helps. In 2009 Harvey Nichols launched a special 'tourist ad campaign' in response to the rise in tourists that occurred due to the fall in the value of the pound. The humorous adverts, highlighting English stereotypes, were written in a number of languages, including Chinese, Arabic, Russian and Brazilian, and were shown in London taxis and specialist tourist magazines. Julia Bowe, Marketing Director for Harvey Nichols commented: 'We believe this series of ads will appeal to the sense of humour of the international customer looking for London's leading selection of fashion, fragrance and food.'

Whatever your interests – fashion, reading, crafts, cooking or technology – it seems that department stores still have, after over 150 years of existence, much to offer. Journalist Susan Hill recently wrote in the *Guardian* newspaper: 'Department stores offer a third way between the misery of trudging the cold, wet high street and purgatorial shopping malls. An hour or three spent in a good department store is balm to the soul.' She's not wrong.

Although up-to-minute in design, the patterned wall of John Lewis's Leicester store is also a subtle reminder of the city's rich textile heritage.

FURTHER READING

Adburgham, A. *Liberty's: A Biography of a Shop*. George Allen & Unwin, 1975.

Briggs, A. *Friends of the People: The Centenary History of Lewis's*. Batsford, 1956.

Briggs, A. *A Social History of England*. Penguin, 1993.

Corina, M. *Fine Silks and Oak Counters: Debenhams 1778–1978*. Century Benham, 1978.

Dale, T. *Harrods: The Store and Legend*. Pan Books, 1986.

Davis, D. *A History of Shopping*. Routledge, 1966.

Draper-Stumm, T. and Kendall, D. *London Shops: The World's Emporium*. English Heritage, 2003.

Ferry, J. W. *A History of the Department Store*. Macmillan, 1960.

Honeycombe, G. *Selfridges: Seventy-Five Years: The Story of the Store, 1909–1984*. Selfridges, 1984.

Lambert, R. S. *The Universal Provider: A Study of William Whiteley and the Rise of the London Department Store*. George G. Harrap, 1938.

Lancaster, B. *The Department Store: A Social History*. Leicester University Press, 1995.

Marwick, A. *British Society Since 1945*. Penguin, 1996.

Miller, M. *The Bon Marché: Bourgeois Culture and the Department Store, 1869–1920*. Princeton University Press, 1994.

Morrison, K. A. *English Shops and Shopping: An Architectural History*. Yale University Press, 2007.

Moss, M. and Turton, A. *A Legend of Retailing: House of Fraser*. Weidenfeld & Nicolson, 1989.

Pasdermadjian, H. *The Department Store: Its Origins, Evolution and Economics*. Newman Books, 1954.

Peel, D. W. *A Garden in the Sky: The Story of Barkers of Kensington, 1870–1857*. W. H. Allen, 1960.

Stobart, J. *Spend, Spend, Spend: A History of Shopping*. The History Press, 2008.

Woodhead, L. *Shopping, Seduction and Mr Selfridge*. Profile Books, 2008.

As the design and advertising copy of this promotional booklet from around 1910 suggest, the Printemps store is 'devoted to women'.

INDEX

Page numbers in italics refer to illustrations

Advertising 20, 21, 23, 26–7, 31, 43, 47, 61–2, *61*
Allders 57
Arnott & Co. 9, 16, 23
Associated Independent Stores 58
Austins 58
Bainbridge's *2*, 9, *9*, 16, *19*, 28
Bakers & Larners 58
Banburys 55
Barkers 10, 15, 23, *29*, 30, 35, 36, 37, 41, 45
Barnes & Co. 30
Beales 41
Bentalls 27
Binns 10, 16, 37, 48
Birmingham 35, 41, 58–9, *59*
Blacklers 57
Bonds *50*
Bon Marché 14, 15, *20*, 27, 28, 37, 39, 48
Boswells 57
Bournemouth 41
Boutiques 43, 45, 57
Bradford 10
Brands and branding 35, 47, 61
Brent Cross 51
Brown's 15, 41
Brown Muff & Co. 10
Camp Hopson 57
Cardiff 10, 31, 33, 37, 48
Cars 5, *25*, 33, *35*, 51
Cash registers *42*, *48*
Cavendish House 10, 15
Chain stores 35
Cheltenham 10, 15
Chester 15, 41
Chiesman's 10
Christmas 5, 27, 32
Colosseum 16
Consumerism 10
Co-operative stores 35
Crinolines 8, *8*, 9
Debenham & Freebody (Debenhams) 10, *17*, 31, *31*, 36, 41, *47*, 51, *54*, 57, *60*, 61
Departments 5, 6, 9, *9*, 10, 11, 15, *20*, 21, *21*, 31, 42, 45, *45*, 46, 50, *50*, 57
Derry & Toms 15, *22*, *29*, 30, 31, 36, 41
D. H. Evans 10, 16, 36
Dickins & Jones 30, 31–2, 36, 42
Dior, Christian 42
Drapers 8, *8*, 9, 10
Eastmond & Co. 55
Edinburgh 10, 15, *28*, 30, *51*, *62*
Eldon Square 53
Electrical goods 5, 33–4, *35*, 50, *50*, 57
Escalators 14, 16, *19*, 21, *40*, *49*, 55, *55*, 56
Fashion 5, 8, 9, 15, *16*, 32, *32*, *33*, 37, *37*, *40*, 42–3, *43*, *44*, *45*, 62
Fenwick's *18*, *24*, *42*, 51, *51*, 53
First World War 31, *31*, 32, 37
Fraser's (House of Fraser) 15, 42, 45, 46, 51, *51*, 57, 60
Galeries Lafayette 14, *14*
Gamages 15, *25*, 26, 27
Glasgow 9, 15, 16, 17, 26, *43*
Great Exhibition of 1851 10–11, *11*
Hancock & Wood 58
Harrods 5, 6, *19*, *20*, 21, 23, 26, 27, 30, 31, 33, 35, *35*, 36, 37, *39*, *40*, 41, 43, 51, 53
Harvey Nichols 36, *61*, 62, *62*
Holdrons 37
Home delivery 30
Howells 5, 10, 31, 33, 37, 48
International Association of Department Stores 41
Jackson's 16, *16*, 21, 58, *58*
Jenners 10, 15, *51*
John Lewis 10, *32*, *34*, 37, *38*, *44*, *48*, 49, *49*, *50*, 51, 53, *53*, 55, 57, 59–61, *62*
Jolly & Son 9
Jones Bros *1*
Kendal, Milne & Faulkner 9
Kensington 10, 15, *29*, 30, 41, 42
Lamson pneumatic tube system 21, *21*, 58
Leicester 59, *62*
Lewis's 5, 15, 17, 23, 35, *36*, 37, 41, 51
Liberty 5, 15, *36*, *46*, 61
Lifts 17, 18, 27
Liverpool 10, 15, 17, 27, 28, 35, *36*, 37, 39, 41, *55*, 57
London 7, 8, 10, 11, 15, 28, 36, 42, 53, 55, 62
Mail order 31
Manchester 7, 9, 35, 41
Marshall & Snelgrove *18*
Maule's 10, *28*, 30
McEwens 10, *10*, *38*, 55, *57*
McDonalds *43*
Middle classes 7, 10, 25
New Look 42, *43*
Newcastle 9, 18, *18*, 24, *42*, 53
Oxford 57
Oxford Street 10, 37, *38*, *44*, *48*, 49, *49*, *50*, *53*, 55
Paris 14–15
Perth 10, *10*, *38*, 55, *57*
Peter Jones 55, *56*
Peter Robinson's 31
Pontings 15, *29*, 36, 41
Pratts 37
Printemps 13, *13*, *63*
Proto-department stores 8, 9
Publicity 27, 61
Quant, Mary 43
Quin & Axten 37
Railways 7, 8
Rationing 38–9, *39*
Reading 16, *16*, *21*, *58*
Roof gardens *29*, 30
Roomes 58
Peter Jones *35*
Sales 5, *22*, *25*, 27, *33*, 42
Second World War 27, 36, *37*, 37–9, 41, 53
Selfridge, Harry Gordon 26–8
Selfridges: 5, 23, *24*, 26, 27, 28, 30, 31, 32, 34, *35*, 37, 46, 51, 55, *56*, 58–60, *59*, 61, *61*; Miss Selfridge 46, *47*; Selfridge Provincial Stores 37
Sheffield 35, 37, 41, 48
Shoplifting 24, 25
Showrooms 5, 7, 10, 15, 16, *19*
Staff: 31; fines 31; holidays 31, 33; hours 31, 32; living-in 31; shortages 41; training 31, *48*; wages 32
Sunderland 10, 16, 36, 37
Suffragettes 30
Swan & Edgar *4*, *33*, 36
Takeovers 36–7, 51
Trewin Brothers *43*
Twiggy *47*
Vans 30, *30*, 31
Victoria, Queen 8
Walsh's 48
Websites 60
Whiteley, William 11, 14, *25*, 27
Whiteley's 11, 13, 16, 37, *37*, 41
Windows 5, 16, 21, 23, *24*, 30, *34*, *53*, 61
Women 5, *25*, 30, *31*, 32, 37, *38*, *39*, 42, 51
Working classes 32, 41
Wylie & Lochhead 17